POET'S FIRST LIGHT

t. kilgore splake

First Edition: 2020
Rs. 200/-

Cyberwit.net
HIG 45 Kaushambi Kunj, Kalindipuram
Allahabad - 211011 (U.P.) India
http://www.cyberwit.net
Tel: +(91) 9415091004 +(91) (532) 2552257
E-mail: info@cyberwit.net

Printed at Thomson Press India Limited.

# # # #

"'i can see clearly now the rain is gone
i can see all obstacles in my way
gone are the dark clouds that had me blind
it's gonna be a bright, bright sunshiny day"

"'i can see clearly now"
johnny nash

"while the day made it fresh claim again upon the
darkness, ..."

richard ford
"sorry for your troubles"

taste of heaven

alone in wilderness
trees sheltering poet
witnessing nature's beauty
early rain shower
morning light clearing
bright rainbow colors
above the earth
decorating the sky

anonymous poet

\# \# \# \#

poet's spirit

floating through pines
pale october light
on brautigan creek currents

\# \# \# \#

reality on mute

housewives of new york
flashing big tits
practicing fake orgasms

\# \# \# \#

texter

doesn't read books
sadly lacking imagination
can't see beyond screen

####

dark ages

suddenly losing power
cellphone wisdom erased
empty new world

####

river of no return

floating away from life
lost in stream currents
leaving memories behind

####

chastity

church wedding ceremony
father of bride free
from saving her virginity

pandemic escape

.357 ego trip
surprising backdoor thieves
gun's final bullet
heaven's prayer

\# \# \# \#

gambler

high roller poet
betting the farm
postage stamp ante

\# \# \# \#

four on the floor

driven poet
criticizing wannabe
idling in park

\# \# \# \#

morning after poetry reading

stale camembert squares
cheap white wine
starving artist's breakfast

\# \# \# \#

wilderness images

sandhill crane silhouettes
sun setting over marshland
shadows like monks praying

\# \# \# \#

robert johnson

traded soul to devil
to play guitar blues
haunting music from hell

\# \# \# \#

jim harrison

last poem on desk
final words never read
passport into heaven

# # # #

leonard cohen

dark midnight voice
echoing in brain
hallelujah sweet hallelujah

# # # #

"little sparrow"

edith driven to sing
giving concert dollars
to paris poor

# # # #

josephine baker

smooth naked rhythms
silky bronze flesh
exotic sexual desire

\# \# \# \#

basquiat

riding on death
rising toward heaven
hot rail whisper

\# \# \# \#

modigliani's women

tiny eyes thin smiles
hiding sad souls
seeing beyond death

\# \# \# \#

cartier-bresson's camera

black and white artistry
avoiding color filming
noisy creative confusion

# # # #

waking to surprise

morning after making love
strange bedmate affair
discovering skin infection
using kwell soap

# # # #

damselflies

electric blue bodies
thin iridescent wings
tiny nymphs floating
over brautigan creek
tempting rainbow feast

# # # #

long white escape

frozen blizzard beauty
purity of blown snow
winter winds creating
soft pine music
path disappearing
poet blessedly lost

\# \# \# \#

graduation

cruising main street
old rusty pickup
graduation cap tassel
hanging from mirror
young teen waiting
jack daniel's epiphany

\# \# \# \#

calendar months

after water broke
hospital c-section
delivery nurse saying
'it's a girl'
counting on fingers
daughter not mine

# # # #

modigliani's midnight canvas

poet's ghost lover
pretty young woman
black dress covering
soft silky flesh
moonlight in her eyes
there for a moment
then suddenly gone

never returning

lighting dry tinder
bright flames exploding
poet again seeking
creative awakening
secret silently vanishing
lost in smoke
cool fire ashes

# # # #

pandemic solution

sig sauer
full metal jackets
.357 surprise
for men gone mad
breaking in backdoor
slipping last cartridge
under his lip
whispering hello mom

# # # #

lonesome

new year's eve
valentine's day celebration
no dates or parties
home watching videos
black and white oldies
dreaming of red hearts
saying 'i love you'
ghost of guy lombardo

\# \# \# \#

signs of winter

late august afternoon
dancing dust motes
fading sunlight shadows
quiet celebration
for autumn's arrival
following bright colors
forest decay
death soon returning
quieting wilderness

\# \# \# \#

murder

wounded squirrel
limping in puckerbrush
shot by drunken professor
almost nighttime
forest becoming dark
chasing it through woods
hoping to end its misery
eliminate my shame
neither of us
dying alone

# # # #

disappointment

graybeard poet
dry wrinkled scrotum
limp fleshy pecker
lost in dreams
of young teenage girls
while older woman
counting calendar months
running out of time
baby making agenda
prince charming vanishing
lost in bedroom shadows

# # # #

summer's over

no more baseball
rawlings glove warping
leather drying out
suddenly worried over
diagramming sentences
latin word declensions
algebra x's and y's
no seventh inning stretch
bottom of ninth rally
home plate catcher
wearing tools of ignorance
seriously wondering
who needs this shit

# # # #

payback

quiet lonely girl
anonymous lost face
toting large bookbag
with textbooks and notes
to regular classroom seat
school days passing
jealous of cheerleaders
lost in pep rally shadows
never having prom date

wearing orchid corsage
began writing poetry
soon creative works
achieving literary fame
suddenly the world
giving her attention

\# \# \# \#

fleeing olga

if wife should ask
getting sunday newspapers
poet's planned reply
speedometer red line rising
pickup gaining speed
passing city limits
nervous eyes glued
to rearview mirror
paranoid brain expecting
mercedes rapidly closing
in hot pursuit
warm beer relaxing
tight steering wheel grip
crossing mackinaw bridge
heart beat slower
welcoming escape

\# \# \# \#

poet's final journey

artist dave engel
close wisconsin friend
administering splake's
last will and testament
climbing rocky trail
reaching cliffs summit
releasing poet's ashes
off granite escarpment
old poet tree location
small pieces of bone
gray crematory powders
scattered to the winds
sustenance for
animals birds insects
also absorbed by earth
nourishing cliffs wilderness
maybe rare remains
carried beyond heaven

\# \# \# \#

life's decision

ludwig trap set
high hat cymbals
drumsticks pounding
steady snare drum rhythms
loud rim shots echoing
on the way to college

master's degree diploma
becoming college professor
early mornings
giving classroom lectures
instead of weekend gigs
small band playing
country-western songs
community square dances
delton township hall
smoky dickens inn
knotty club bar
now burnt out musicians
waiting last call

# # # #

owl called my name

past middle-aged professor
having lost his way
wondering if life gets better
lost in campfire trance
watching logs disappear
becoming glowing embers
soon hot white coals
noticing something moving
dark tree shadows
piercing yellow eyes
staring out of darkness
huge wilderness owl
becoming nighttime companion

providing creative wisdom
dark soft feathers
muffling evening sounds
silently floating away
through tree branches
suddenly gone

# # # #

part of the world

ophthalmologist appointment
checking blurred vision
discovering glaucoma
optic nerve damaged
fading loss of sight
now daily climbing cliffs
walking brautigan creek banks
absorbing wilderness beauty
so blind poet remembers
warm ice out sun
melting away winter
cold spring rains
nourishing trees and wildflowers
light forest breeze
creating beautiful music
summer storms exploding
exciting thunder and lightning
rainbow shortly after
feeling butterflies flitting
soft red autumn leaves

later warped brown shapes
pink and green shadows
fall northern lights
dancing across sky
before quiet arctic chill
winter season of long white

# # # #

gwyneth

suddenly awake
from deep serious dream
staring into morning
peach and violet hues
lighting eastern horizon
feeling urgent need
to pack a few things
fill truck with petrol
turn highway miles west
escaping keweenaw peninsula
rusting copper mining ruins
with dark original beauty
climbing rocky mountains
hiking new forest trails
chasing fat rainbows
fishing different streams
sadly leaving behind
woman loved
innocent young girl

like johannes vermeer's
"girl with the pearl earring"
soft smooth skin
haunting inviting eyes
her lips hiding secrets
local café barista
always nervously teasing hair
describing life as "chill"
recent romantic memories
boyfriend love letters
long diary scribblings
dried prom orchid corsage
not so long ago
playing with dolls
having first period
suddenly her heart
captured by older man
quiet graybeard poet
drinking morning espressos
wrestling crossword puzzles
window table shadows
may-september connection
whether scandal or relationship
suddenly immediate issue
center of small town gossip
many strongly suggesting
gray grizzled geezer
be branded sexual predator
for jailbait affair
yet during poet's life
never playing things safe
always chasing his passions
risking everything for love

however time running out
obituary shadows near
deciding to abandon
his calumet home
old mining row house
in tamarack location
quickly collecting
toothbrush and underwear
cardboard box of paperbacks
favorite brautigan titles
beckett's "waiting for godot"
clothes in paper sacks
leaving computers behind
along with several printers
snaky mess of cables
free of technologies
finding new place to write
dark wilderness corner
porcupine mountains retreat
old log cabin
drummond island escape
new village stranger
felch or amasa
living in old church
vacant school house
scribbling final biography
green memo books
remembering young gwyneth
her girlhood left behind
becoming a woman
getting her shit together
waiting new love

# # # #

poet's thank you

for papa and jim harrison

graybeard poet appreciation
for many exciting stories
found in their books
sharing hem's adventures
corrida bullfighting spectator
drinking spanish wine
emptying leather bota
watching matador's kill
given tail and ear
sailing gulfstream currents
hemingway's 'pilar' pursuing
magnificent marlin and sailfish
african safaris
hunting wild beasts
trophy heads hanging
on writing room walls
exciting war stories
ambulance driver
italian army volunteer
"battle of caporetto"
"farewell to arms"
colonel cantwell's memories
hurtgen forest terror
battle of the bulge
world war two
buying drinks at sloppy joes
key west florida
poppa dobles favorite

el floridita special
havana club bar
starving artist writer
apartment over sawmill
sweet paris memories
serious 'moveable feast'
ketchum idaho summers
spending many days
staring past sawtooths
decisively ending his life
acting with simple grace
harrison's best books
reflections of life's journey
in 'wolf' memoirs
describing death and redemption
'returning to earth'
poems about growing old
'in search of small gods'
besides serious writing
frequently hunting and fishing
taking long wilderness hikes
with favorite dogs
enjoyed flirting with women
good looking waitresses
pocket flask never empty
full of high octane vodka
chain-smoking unfiltered camels
gourmet for fine foods
grand marais sportsman bar
menu special
baked hard-crust pizzas
over wood fired oven
wilderness evening feasts

cans of spam
shots of hot jack daniel's
heinz variety of beans
shots of hot jack
warm evening companion
for campfire dessert
alone writing poetry
when big muscle blew
soul now beyond heaven
his spirit found
in bears and wolves
beautiful rainbow trout
harrison's ghost shadows
in bright spring trilliums
blazing autumn colors
dancing with heikki lunta
happily celebrating
fierce winter blizzards
michigan's upper peninsula
season of long white

\# \# \# \#

odyssey

graybeard poet's spirit
making important choice
leaving cliffs sanctuary
basic bardic home
journeying with mishipeshu
dark underwater panther
floating on gentle

brautigan creek currents
joining gratiot river
at phoenix location
passing greenland cemetery
ancient gray tombstones
copper mining ghosts
beyond eagle river
into larger lake superior
moving along rocky shoreline
leaving behind
eagle and copper harbors
top of the peninsula
slowly turning eastward
waving quiet hello
to manitou point light
on gray granite shoal
around keweenaw bay
baraga and l'anse distant
pausing at big bay
remembering robert voelker
"anatomy of murder" fame
on south to marquette
resting below old ore dock
remembering beach picnic
playing in sand
with young daughter
of woman i loved
late evening hours
lost in cemetery darkness
looking for her father's grave
moving on to munising
bending around grand island
silently saluting
loren graham's north light
enjoying nature's rare beauty

along rocky shoreline
fantastic sandstone hues
pausing seven-mile creek
where brook trout fishing
with young son ted
several lifetimes ago
arriving at chapel beach
where early each may
arctic body experience
swimming in superior waters
celebration of life
also warm memories
making love with olga
chapel rock shadows
later passing sable dunes
sandy desert expanse
strange distant place
where strange things happen
leaving grand marais behind
spending short moment
at big two-hearted waters
mysterious hemingway river
later listening for voices
coast guard surfboaters
vermillion life-saving station
rowing into waves
fighting stormy tempests
to save seamen lives
at crisp point
watching ford bronco
in four-wheel drive
escaping deep beach sand
pausing at whitefish point

whispering quiet prayer
honoring edmund fitzgerald
lost lake superior ghosts
traveling farther north
reaching michipicoten island
underwater panther's home
warm welcome return
establishing safe harbor
quiet shallow inlet
waiting coming winter
season of long white
running with wolves
chasing woodland caribou
enjoying special holiday
warm homecoming feast
celebrating long journey

\# \# \# \#